Animal Diaries
Life Cycles

A Frog's Life

by
Ellen Lawrence

Consultants:

Suzy Gazlay, MA
Recipient, Presidential Award for Excellence in Science Teaching

Dr. Kerry Kriger
Ecologist; Executive Director and Founder of Save the Frogs!, Santa Cruz, California

Kimberly Brenneman, PhD
National Institute for Early Education Research, Rutgers University, New Brunswick, New Jersey

BEARPORT
PUBLISHING

New York, New York

Credits

Cover, © Cathy Keifer/Shutterstock; Cover L, © Harry Rogers/Science Photo Library; 2, © Gerald A. DeBoer/Shutterstock; 4T, © Superstock; 4B, © Yurly Kulyk/Shutterstock; 5, © Kris Holland/Shutterstock; 6, © Carolina Biological/Corbis; 6–7, © Gregory K. Scott/Science Photo Library; 8T, © Shutterstock; 8B, © Brandon Alms/Shutterstock; 9, © Michael Durham/FLPA; 10, © Gary Nafis; 10–11, © Harry Rogers/Science Photo Library; 12, © John Mitchell/Science Photo Library; 13T, © David M. Dennis/Animals Animals; 13B, © David M. Dennis/Animals Animals; 15T, © Bruce MacQueen/Shutterstock; 15B, © Gerald A. DeBoer/Shutterstock; 16, © Superstock; 17, © Superstock; 17T, © Jason Patrick Ross/Shutterstock; 18T, © Geoffrey Kuchera/Shutterstock; 18B, © John Pickles/Alamy; 19, © Gary Meszaros/Corbis; 20T, © Yurly Kulyk/Shutterstock; 20B, © Joel Bilt/Shutterstock; 21, © Nature Picture Library; 22L, © Shutterstock; 22TR, © Marek R. Swadzba/Shutterstock; 22BR, © Rene Krekels/FLPA; 23TL, © Bruce MacQueen/Shutterstock; 23TR, © Harry Rogers/Science Photo Library; 23BL, © Nature Picture Library; 23BR, © Jo Crebbin/Shutterstock.

Publisher: Kenn Goin
Editorial Director: Adam Siegel
Creative Director: Spencer Brinker
Design: Alix Wood
Editor: Mark J. Sachner
Photo Researcher: Ruby Tuesday Books Ltd

Library of Congress Cataloging-in-Publication Data

Lawrence, Ellen, 1967–
    A frog's life / by Ellen Lawrence.
        p. cm. — (Animal diaries: Life cycles)
    Includes bibliographical references and index.
    ISBN-13: 978-1-61772-412-1 (library binding)
    ISBN-10: 1-61772-412-2 (library binding)
    1. Frogs—Life cycles—Juvenile literature. I. Title.
    QL668.E2L35 2013
    597.8'9—dc23
                                2011043252

For more information, write to Bearport Publishing Company, Inc., 45 West 21st Street, Suite 3B, New York, New York 10010. Printed in the United States of America in North Mankato, Minnesota.

10 9 8 7 6 5 4 3 2 1

Contents

Name: _Jay_____ Date: _April 15_

Noises in the Night

Tonight I heard loud noises coming from the pond near my house.

It sounded like snoring!

My dad said it was male leopard frogs calling female frogs to the pond.

It's spring, so it's time for the frogs to **mate** and lay eggs.

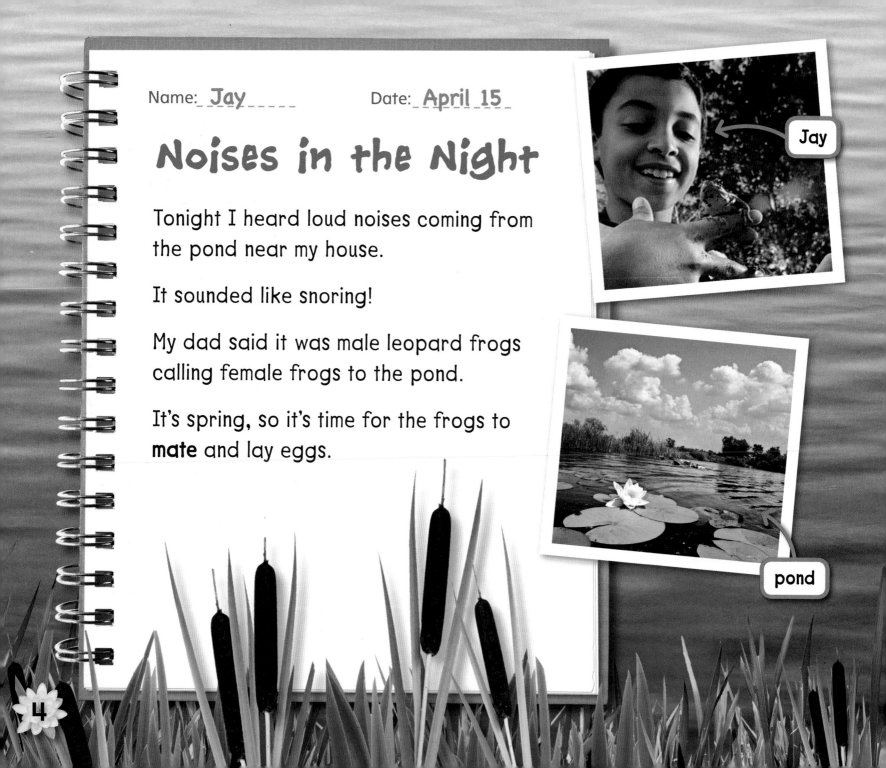

Jay

pond

An adult leopard frog weighs just over one ounce (28 g). That's as heavy as five quarters.

leopard frog

Describe what a leopard frog looks like.

Looking for Eggs

This morning I went to the pond before school.

Wow! The female frogs had laid their eggs during the night.

Floating in the water were big blobs that looked like clear jelly.

Inside each blob of jelly were hundreds of black dots.

Each tiny black dot was a frog egg!

In real life, the eggs are the size of these dots.

a close-up photo of a leopard frog egg

jelly

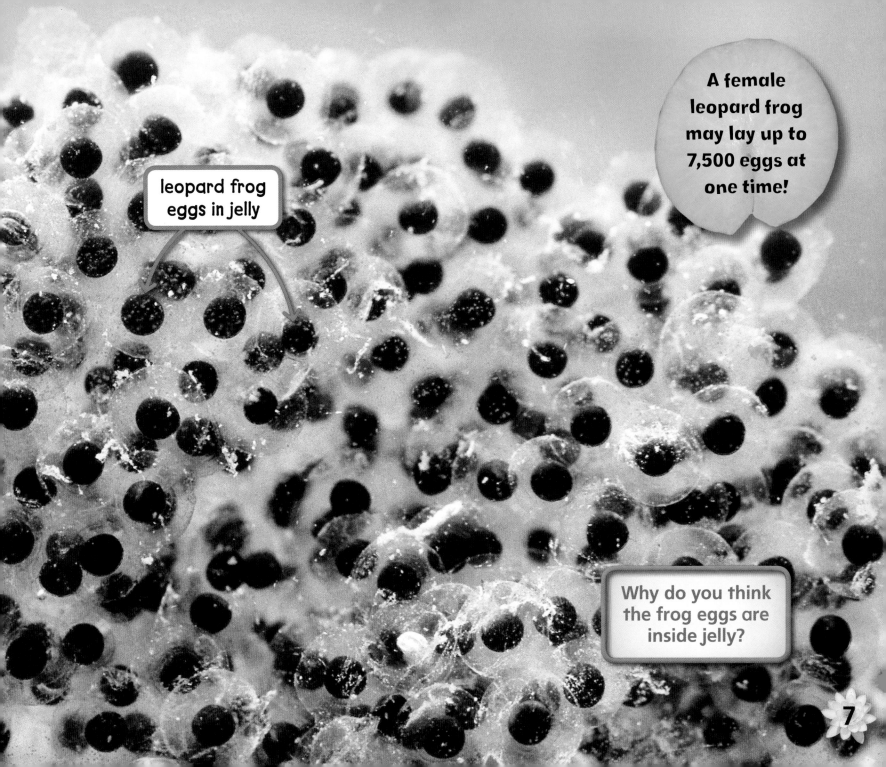

Date: April 30

Eggs in Danger!

The eggs have been in the pond for two weeks.

It's been a dangerous time!

Fish, turtles, newts, leeches, and insects all eat frog eggs.

Luckily, the jelly around the eggs helps to protect them.

It makes it harder for some **predators** to quickly swallow the tiny eggs.

leech

newt

The jelly also protects the delicate eggs from being squashed.

turtle

Date: May 4

Tadpoles

The frogs laid their eggs 18 days ago.

Today, baby frogs called tadpoles hatched from the eggs!

The tadpoles have big heads and long tails.

They look more like fish than frogs!

The tadpoles have body parts called **gills** that help them breathe underwater.

one-day-old tadpoles

In what ways is a leopard frog tadpole different from an adult frog?

Date: July 6

Amazing Changes

I've watched the tadpoles swimming in the pond every day.

Their bodies keep changing.

At first they grew bigger and longer.

Then, at five weeks old, they began to grow back legs.

A week later, front legs started to appear.

Now the tadpoles are nine weeks old.

They look like tiny frogs with tails!

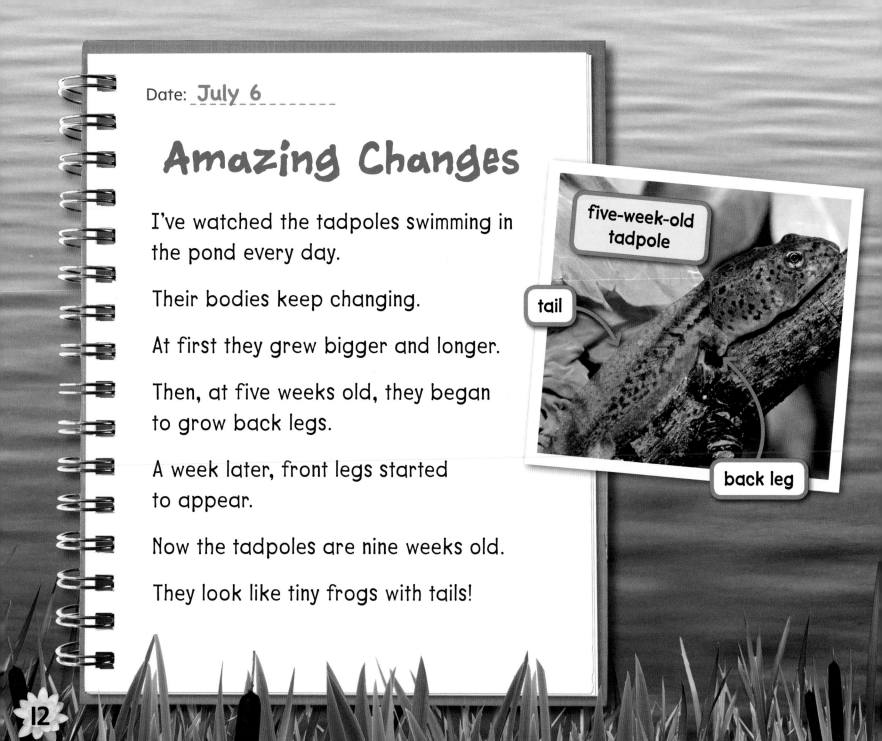

five-week-old tadpole

tail

back leg

seven-week-old tadpole

tail

back leg

front leg

Leopard frog tadpoles may only be about half an inch (1.3 cm) long when they hatch. They can grow to three inches (7.6 cm) long.

nine-week-old tadpole

tail

front leg

back leg

Date: July 27

Meet a Froglet

The tadpoles hatched 12 weeks ago.

Their tails kept getting shorter and shorter—and now they are gone!

The tadpoles have become tiny, young frogs called **froglets**.

They have grown body parts called lungs, for breathing air.

Their lungs have taken the place of their gills.

Now the froglets can leave the water and live on land.

Tadpoles eat mainly water plants. When they become froglets, they eat tiny animals such as insects.

froglet

This froglet and adult frog are life-size. Use a ruler to measure and compare the lengths of their bodies.

adult frog

Date: **October 15**

A Lucky Escape

It's fall and the frogs are now fully grown.

They have to be careful, however.

Fish, birds, snakes, foxes, and raccoons often eat frogs.

This evening, I saw a raccoon trying to catch a frog that was sitting on a rock.

The frog escaped by leaping into the pond.

It jumped about six feet (1.8 m)!

A leopard frog can hide from predators among plants. Its skin color and spots make it hard to see.

Try to find the leopard frogs in these pictures.

17

Date: October 20

Frog Food

Frogs hunt on land for other animals to eat.

Today, I saw a frog catch a dragonfly.

The frog shot its long, sticky tongue out of its mouth.

The dragonfly stuck to the tongue.

Then the frog ate it.

It all happened in less than a second!

dragonfly

a frog eating
a dragonfly

Leopard frogs
eat insects, spiders,
snails, slugs, and
worms. They may also
eat small birds and
other frogs.

Date: **December 15**

Waiting for Spring

It's winter, and the frogs are lying on the mud at the bottom of the pond.

It is warmer there than at the top of the pond.

The frogs will stay in the pond until the weather warms up in spring.

In April, it will be time for the frogs to mate.

The male frogs that hatched this year will be in the pond, calling for females.

the pond in winter

male frogs in the pond

leopard frogs meeting to mate

A leopard frog can live for up to eight years.

Science Lab

A Frog's Life Cycle

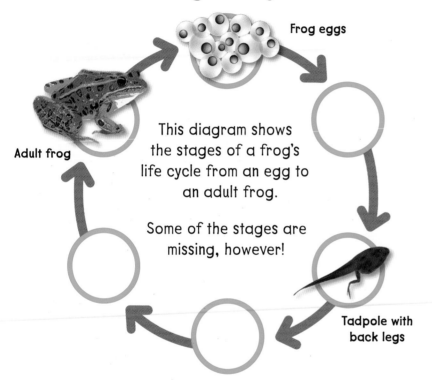

Frog eggs

Adult frog

This diagram shows the stages of a frog's life cycle from an egg to an adult frog.

Some of the stages are missing, however!

Tadpole with back legs

Draw your own diagram of the life cycle in a notebook. Add the missing pictures below in the correct places.

 Tadpole with back and front legs

 Froglet

 Tadpole

(The answer to this activity is on page 24.)

22

— Fact File —

Amphibians

Frogs belong to a group of animals called amphibians.

Salamanders, newts, and toads are also amphibians.

Most amphibians begin their lives in water.

As adults, they usually spend a lot of their time on land.

young newt

adult salamander

Science Words

The tadpole's gills are under here.

froglets (FROG-lits) small frogs that have recently developed from tadpoles

gills (GILZ) body parts that tadpoles and other underwater animals, such as fish, use for breathing

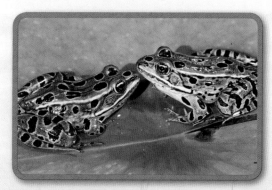

mate (MAYT) to come together in order to have young

predators (PRED-uh-turz) animals that hunt and eat other animals

Index

Read More

Carney, Elizabeth. *Frogs! (National Geographic Readers)*. Washington, D.C.: National Geographic (2009).

Lunis, Natalie. *Green Tree Frogs: Colorful Hiders (Disappearing Acts)*. New York: Bearport (2010).

Zoehfeld, Kathleen Weidner. *From Tadpole to Frog*. New York: Scholastic (2011).

Learn More Online

To learn more about frogs, visit **www.bearportpublishing.com/AnimalDiaries**

Answers

Correct frog life cycle diagram for page 22

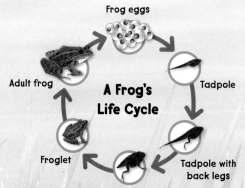

Frog eggs

Tadpole

Tadpole with back legs

Tadpole with back and front legs

Froglet

Adult frog

A Frog's Life Cycle

About the Author

Ellen Lawrence lives in the United Kingdom. Her favorite books to write are those about animals. In fact, the first book Ellen bought for herself, when she was six years old, was the story of a gorilla named Patty Cake that was born in New York's Central Park Zoo.